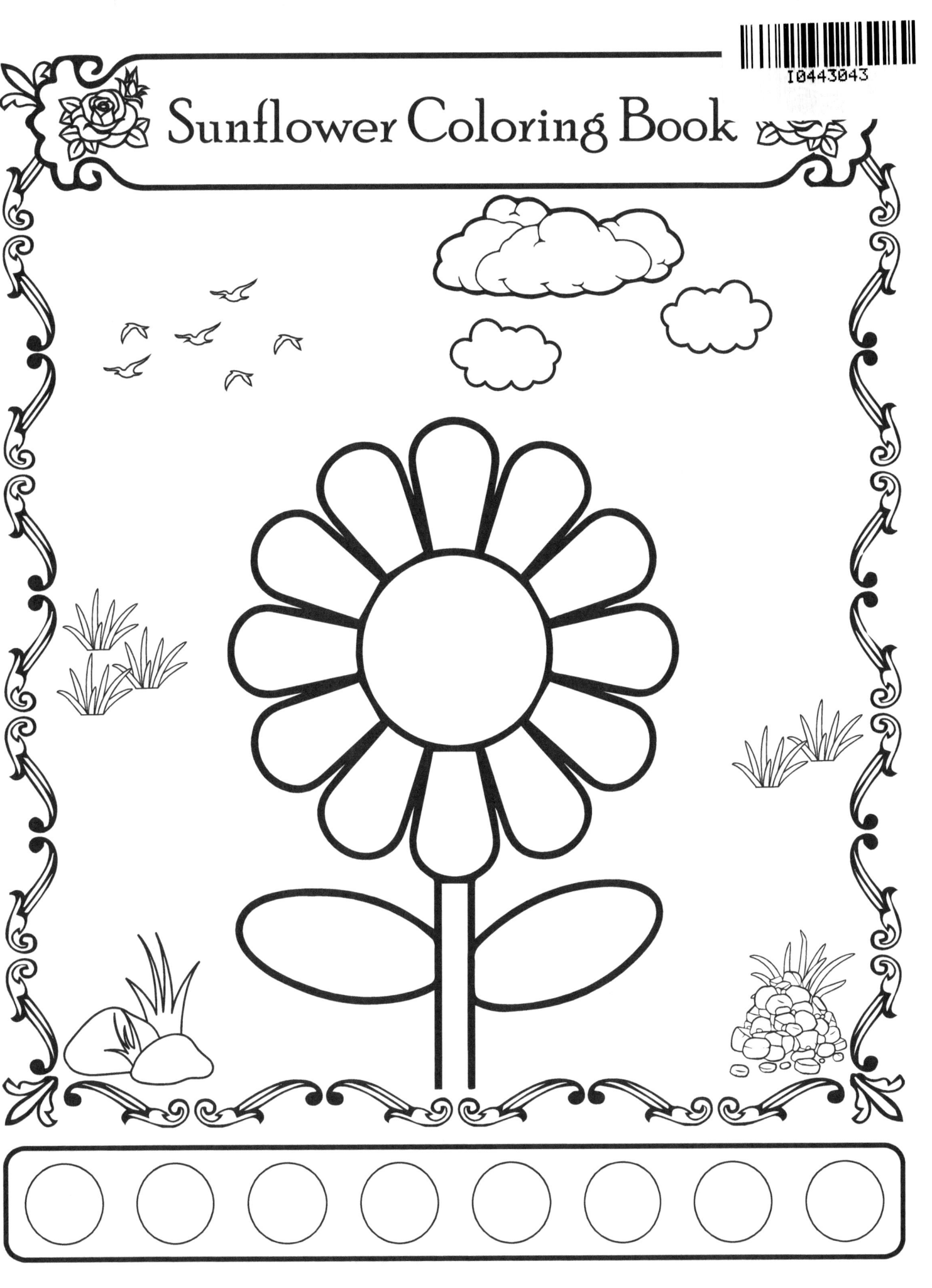

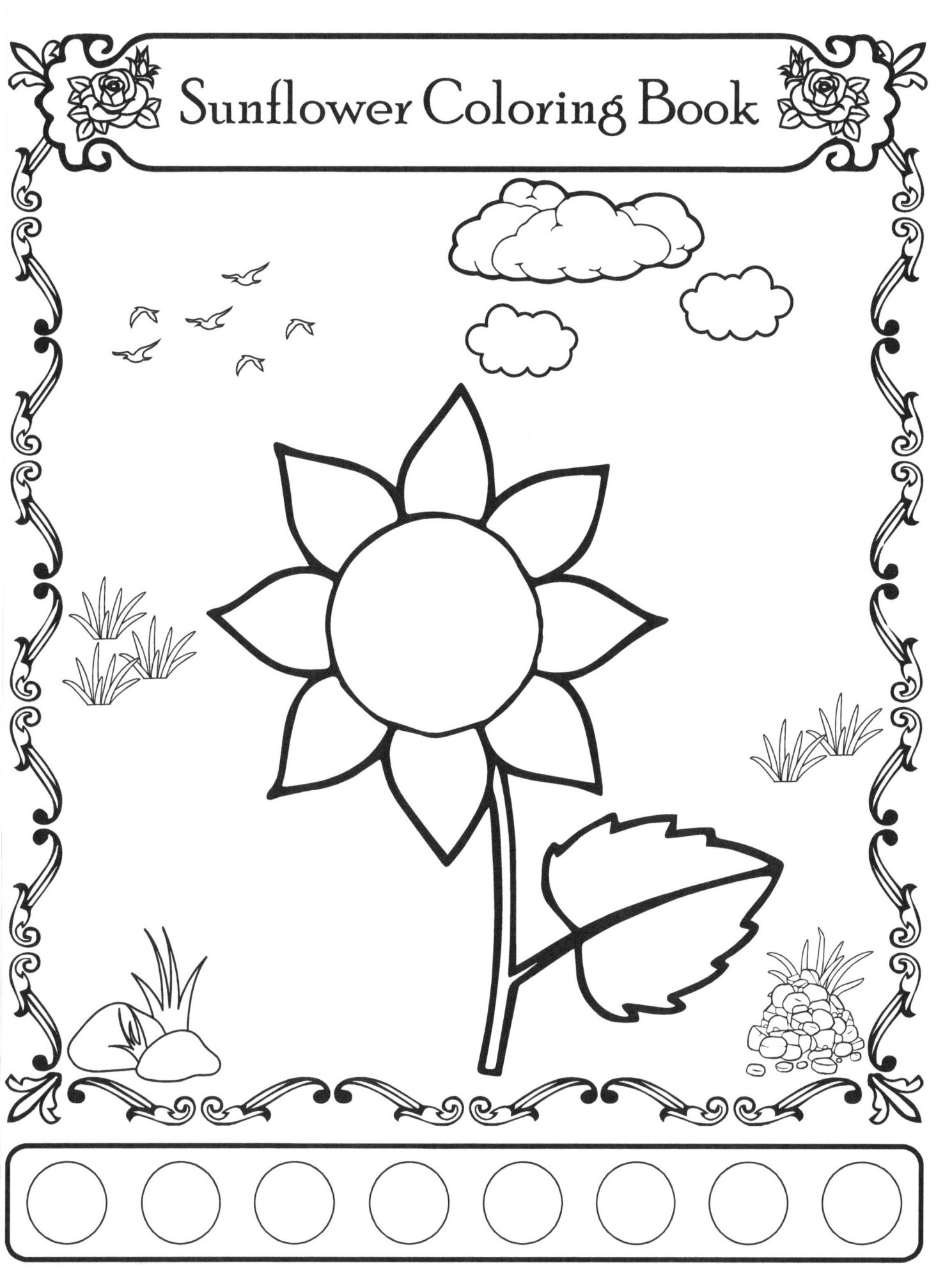

Sunflower Coloring Book

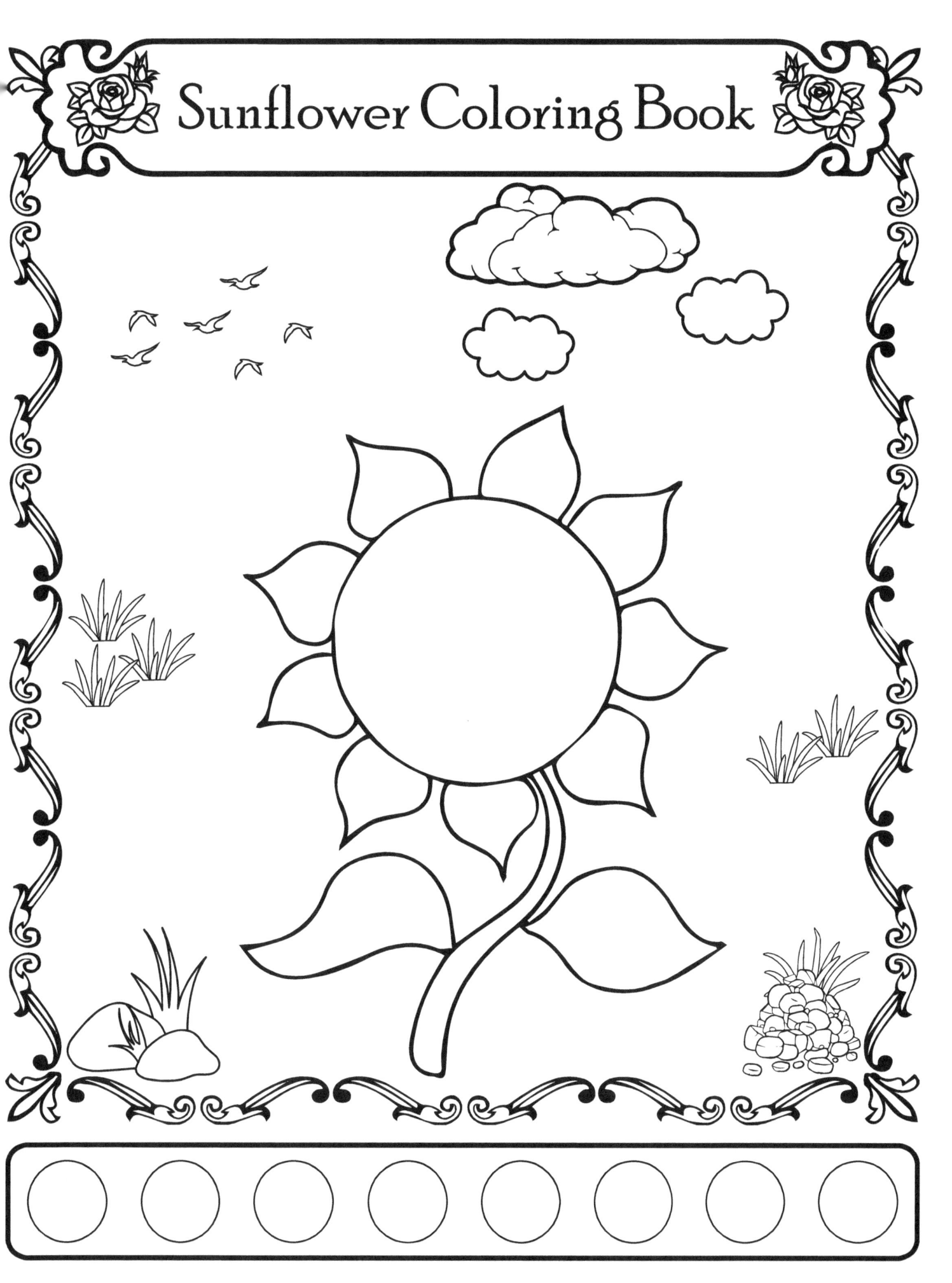

Sunflower Coloring Book

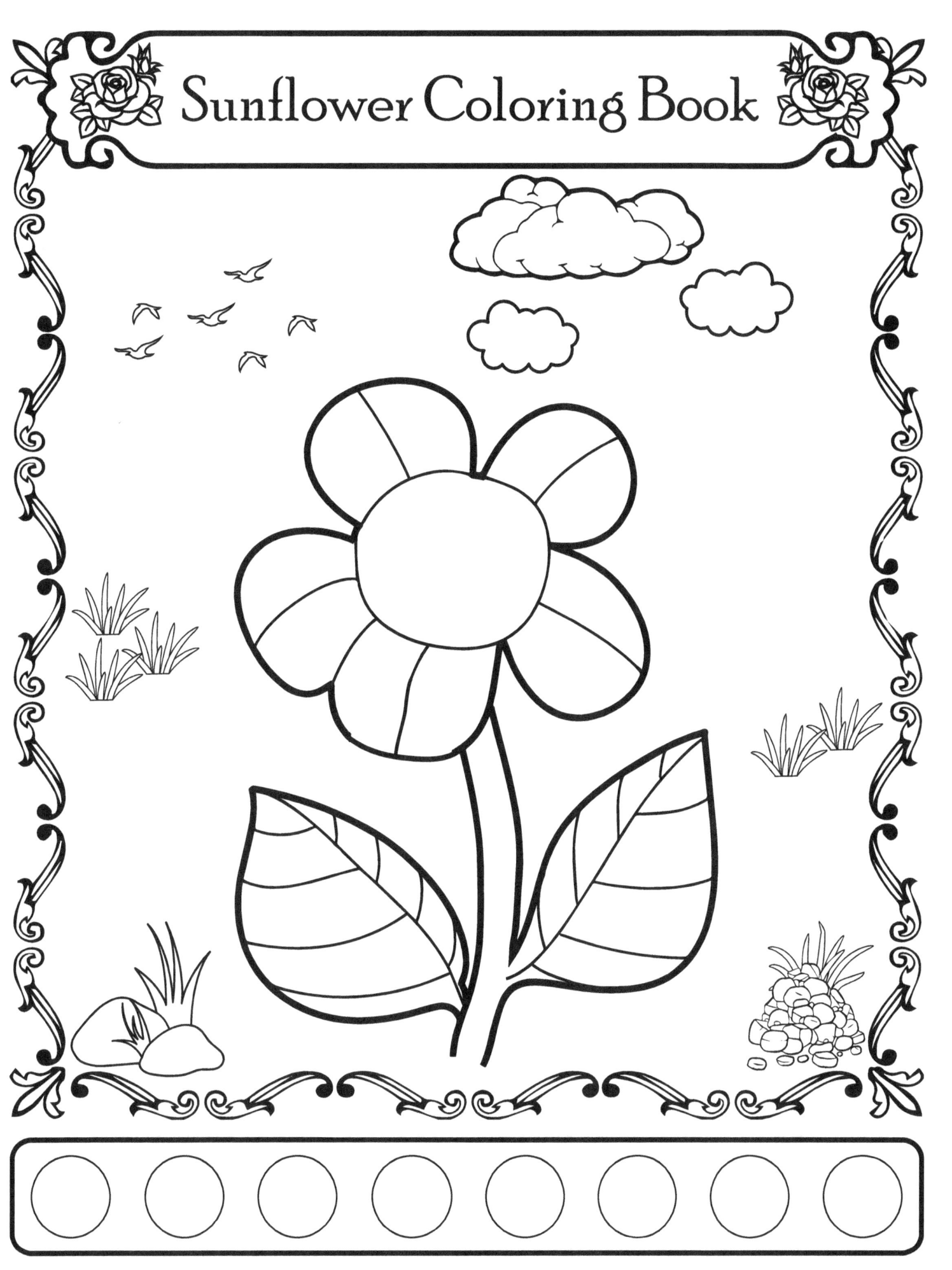

Sunflower Coloring Book

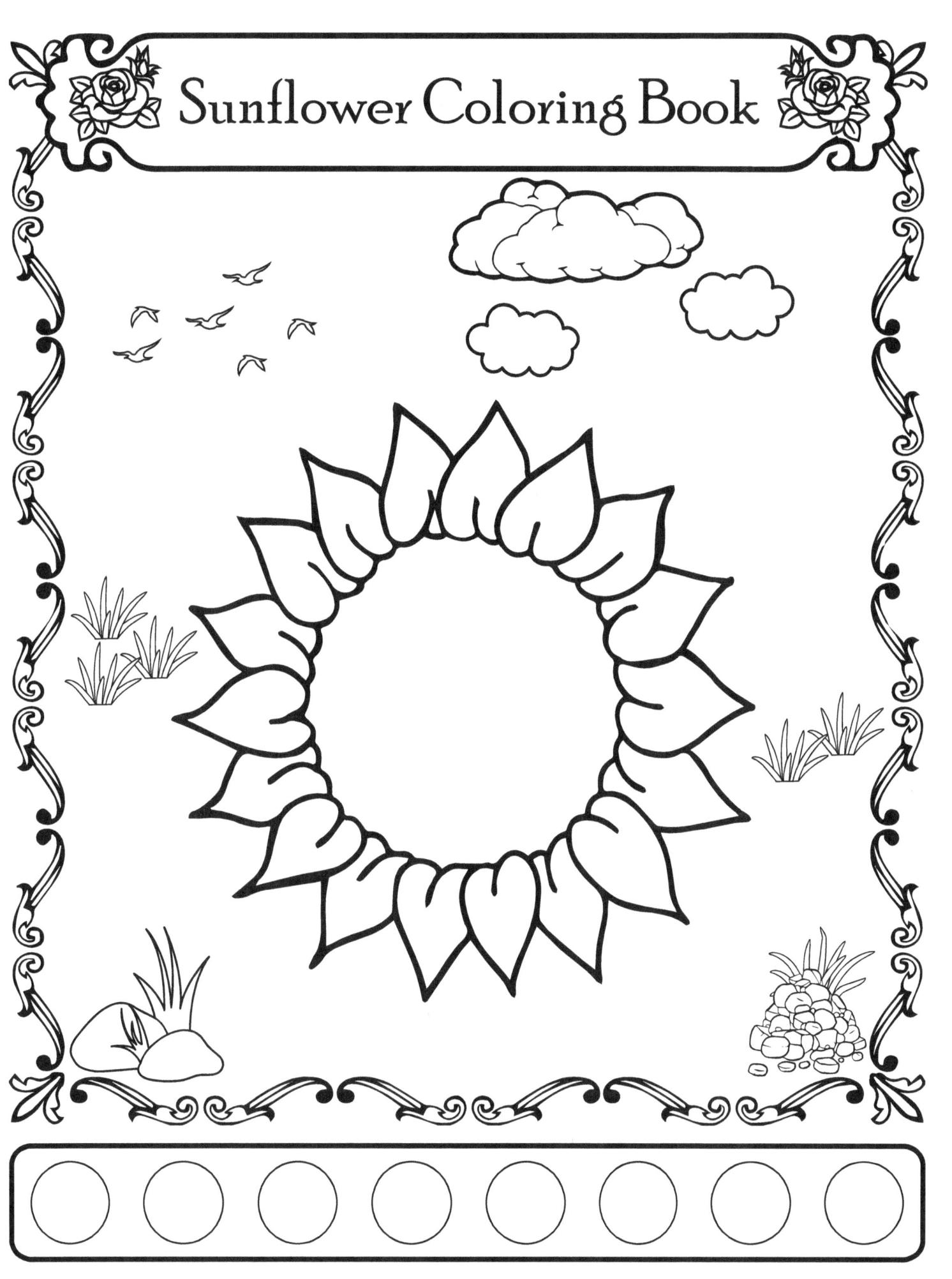

Sunflower Coloring Book

Sunflower Coloring Book

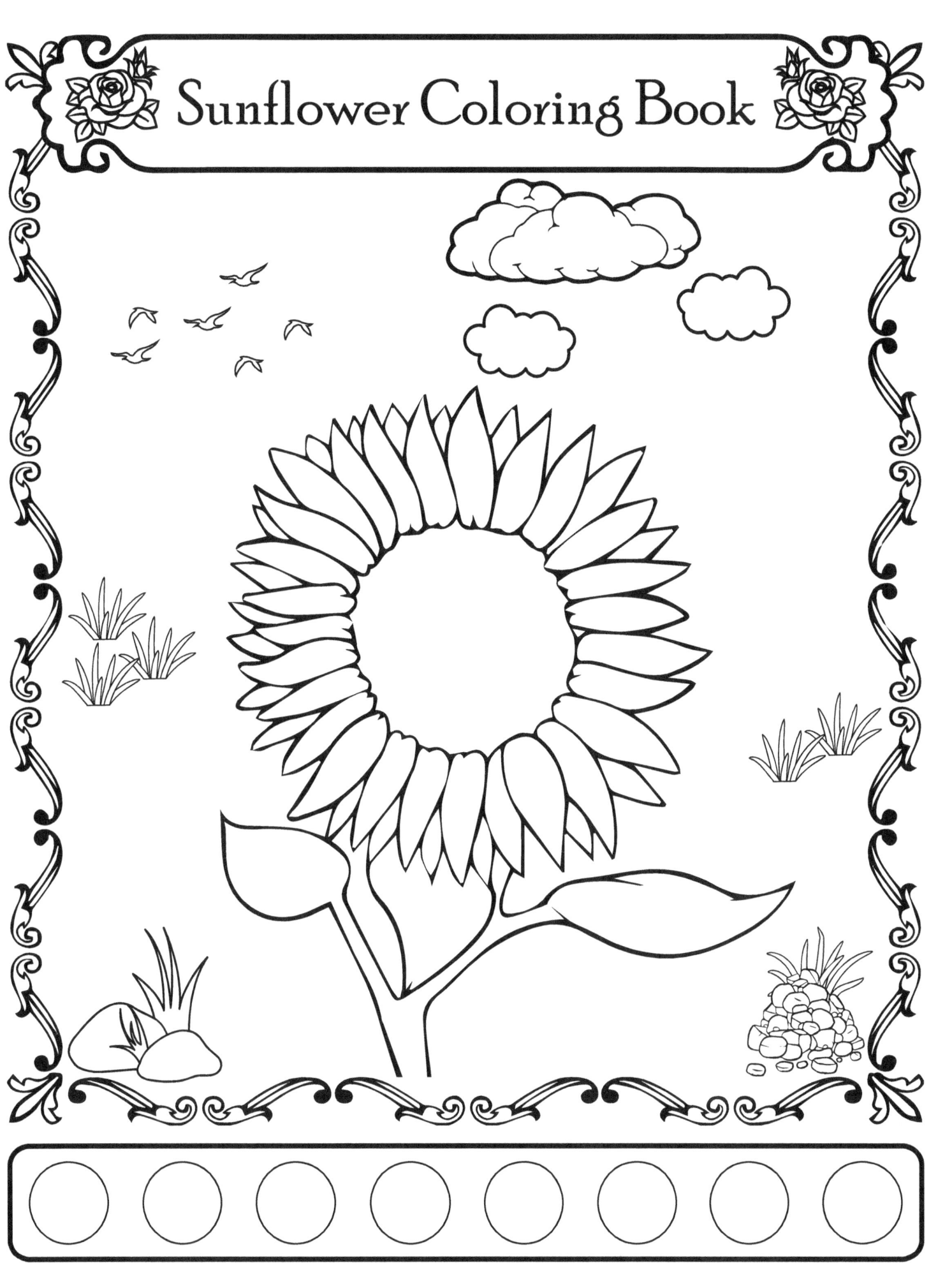

Sunflower Coloring Book

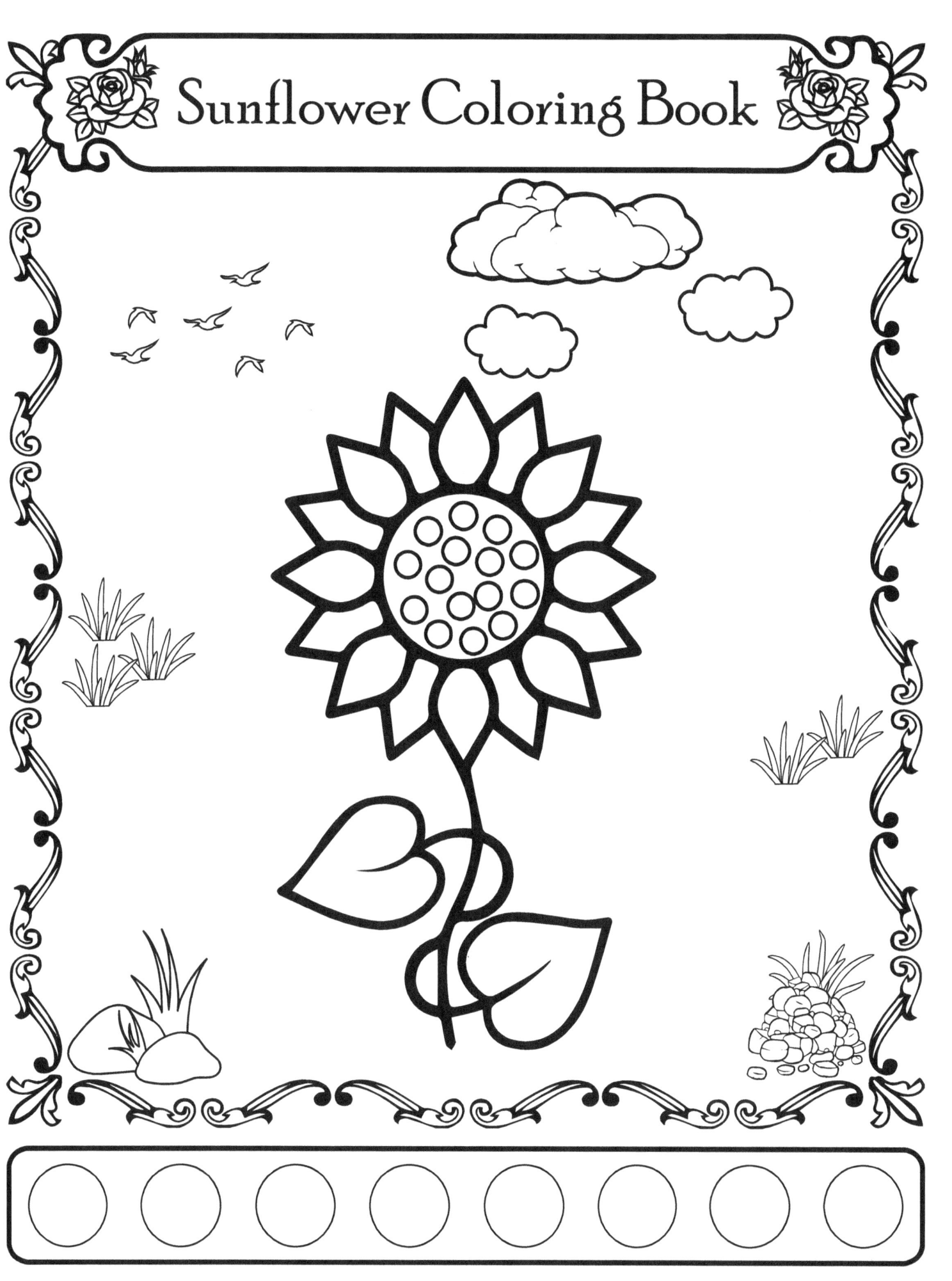

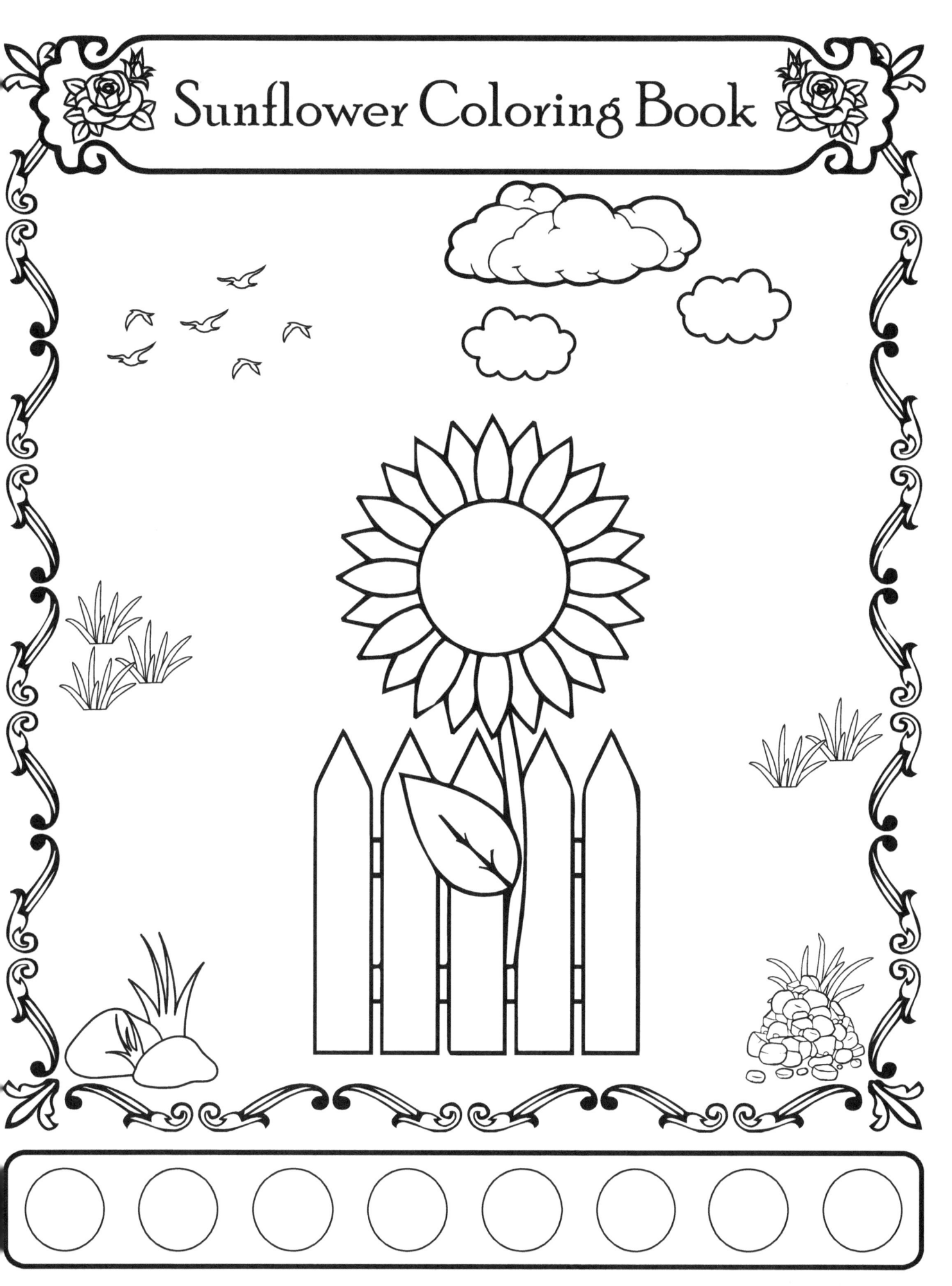

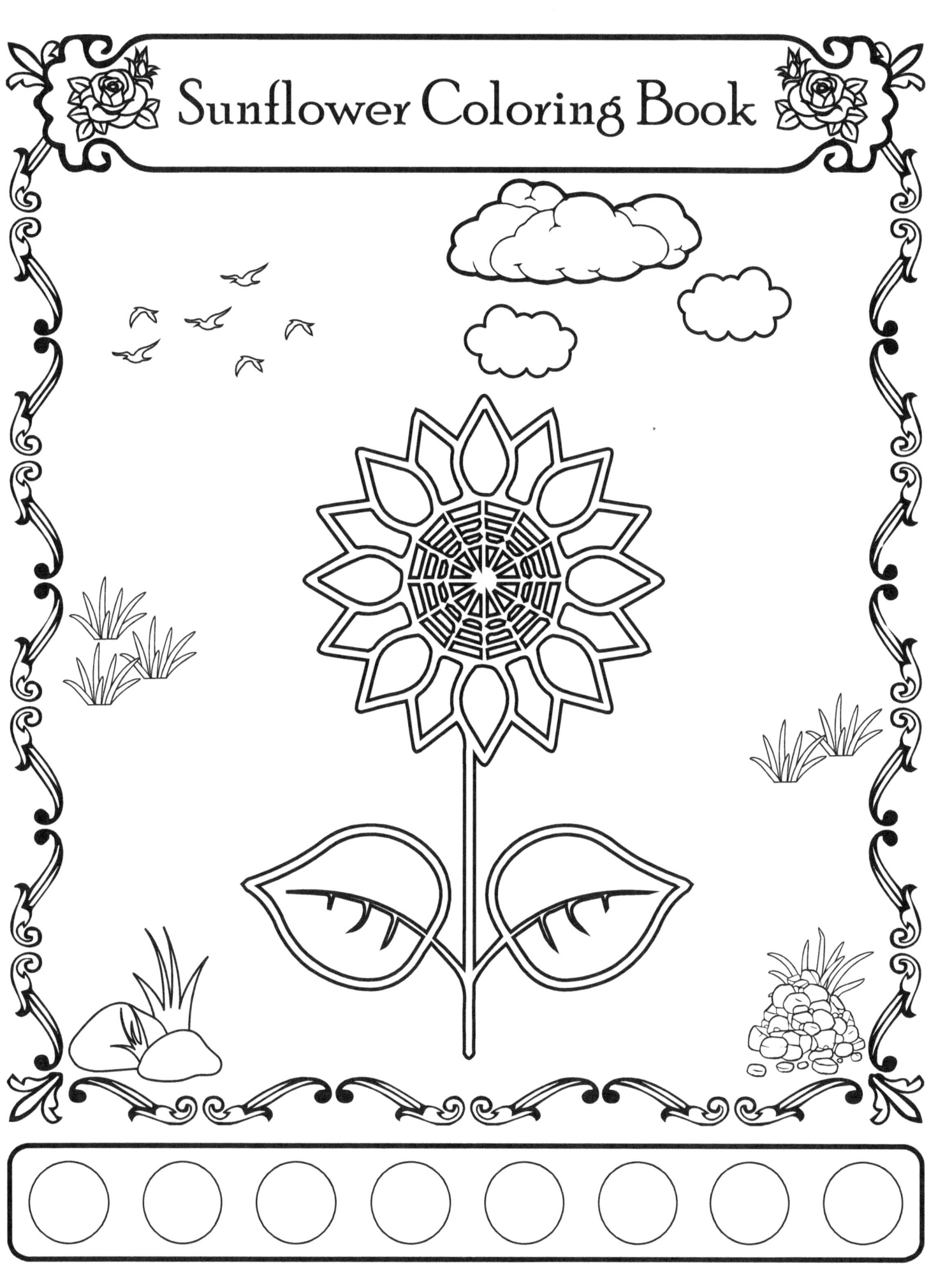

Sunflower Coloring Book

Sunflower Coloring Book

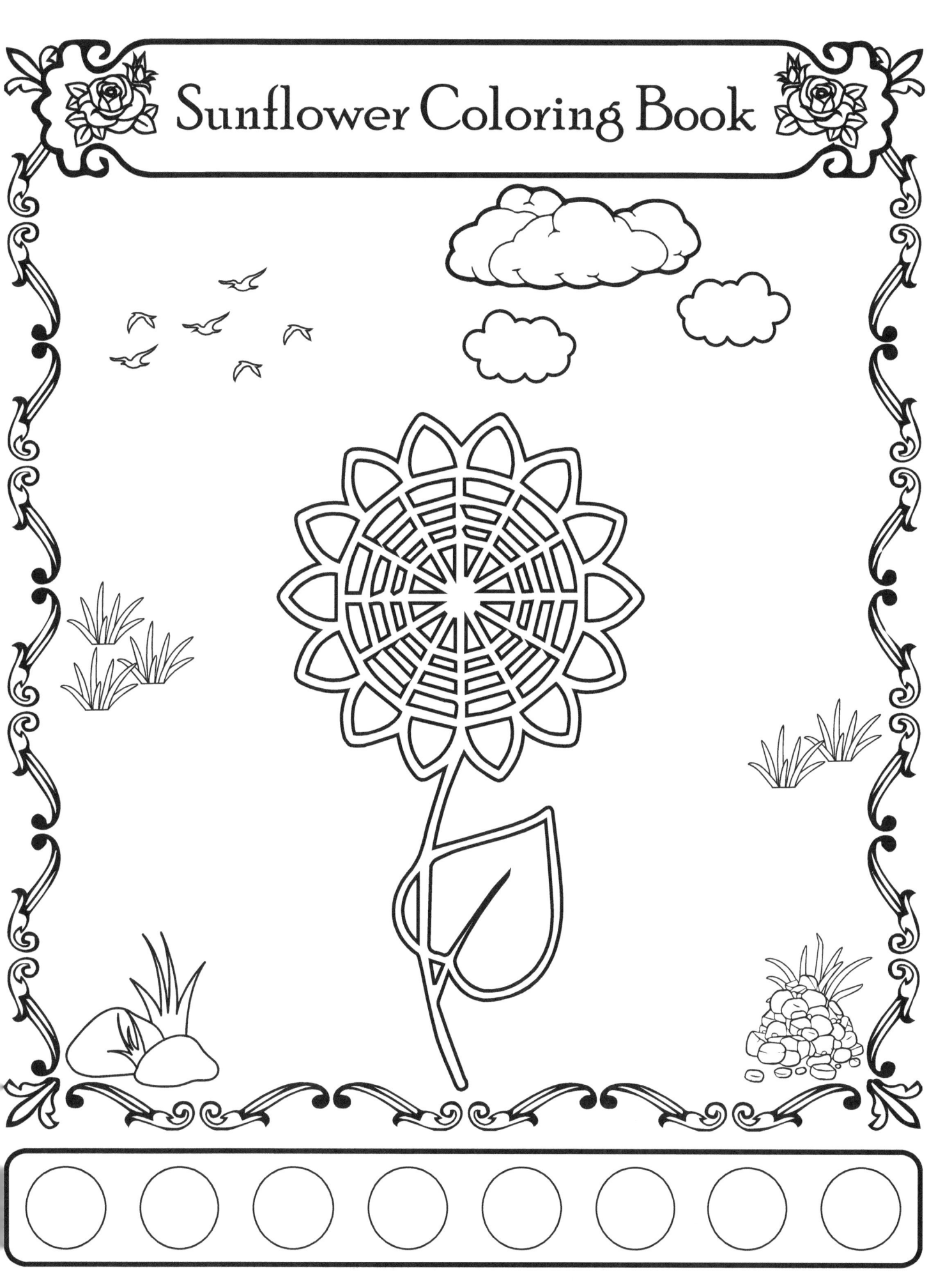

Sunflower Coloring Book

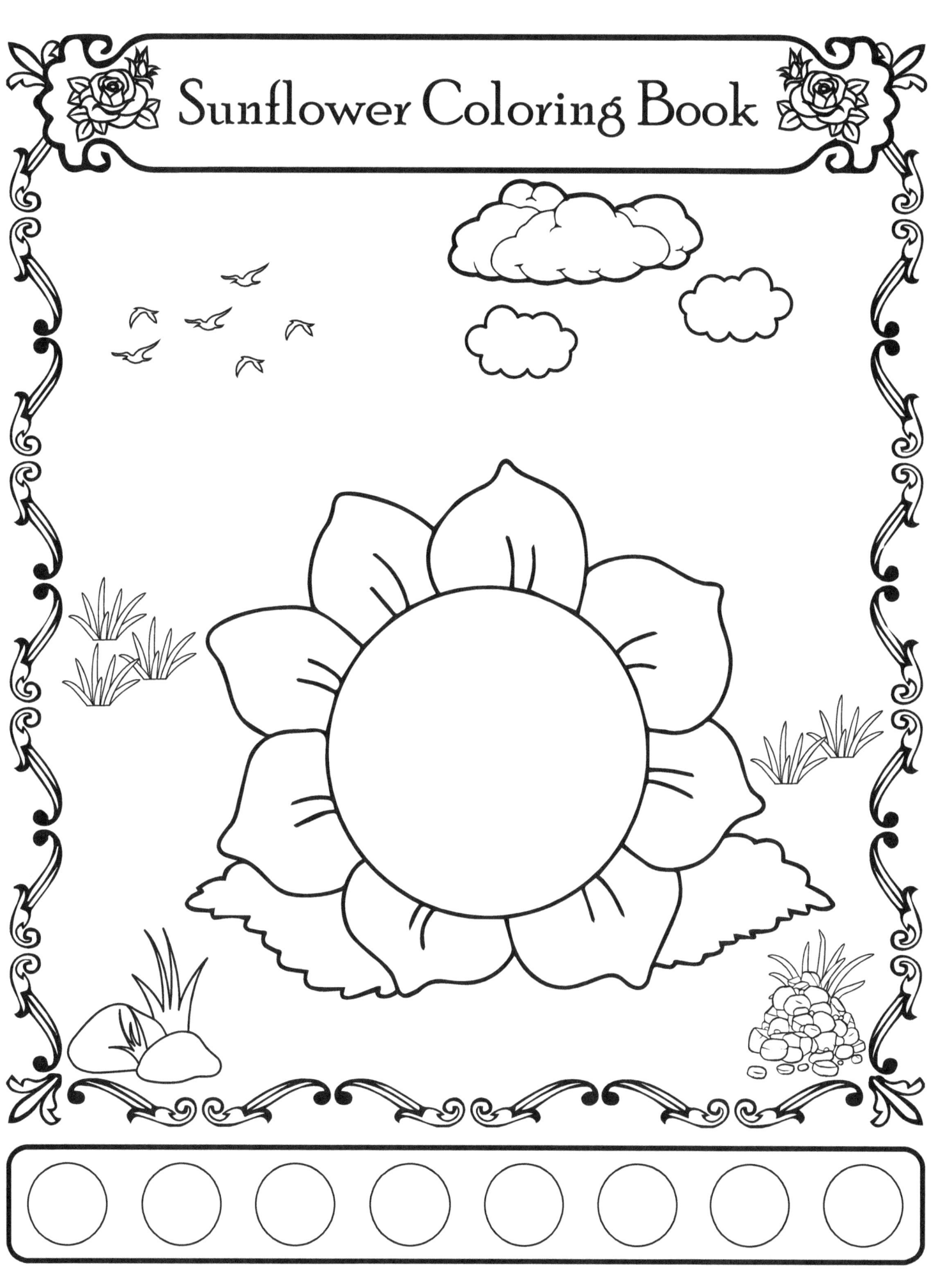

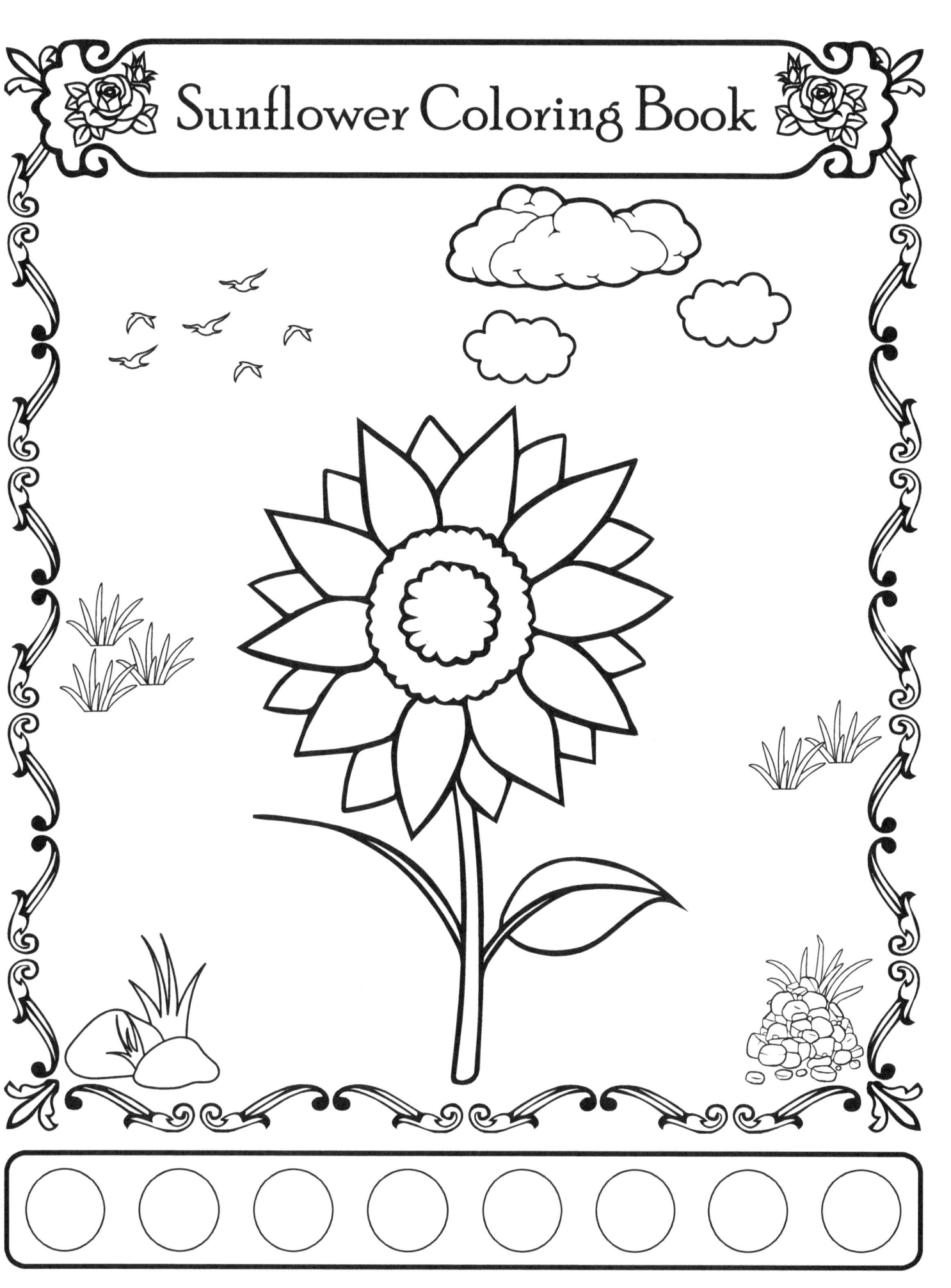

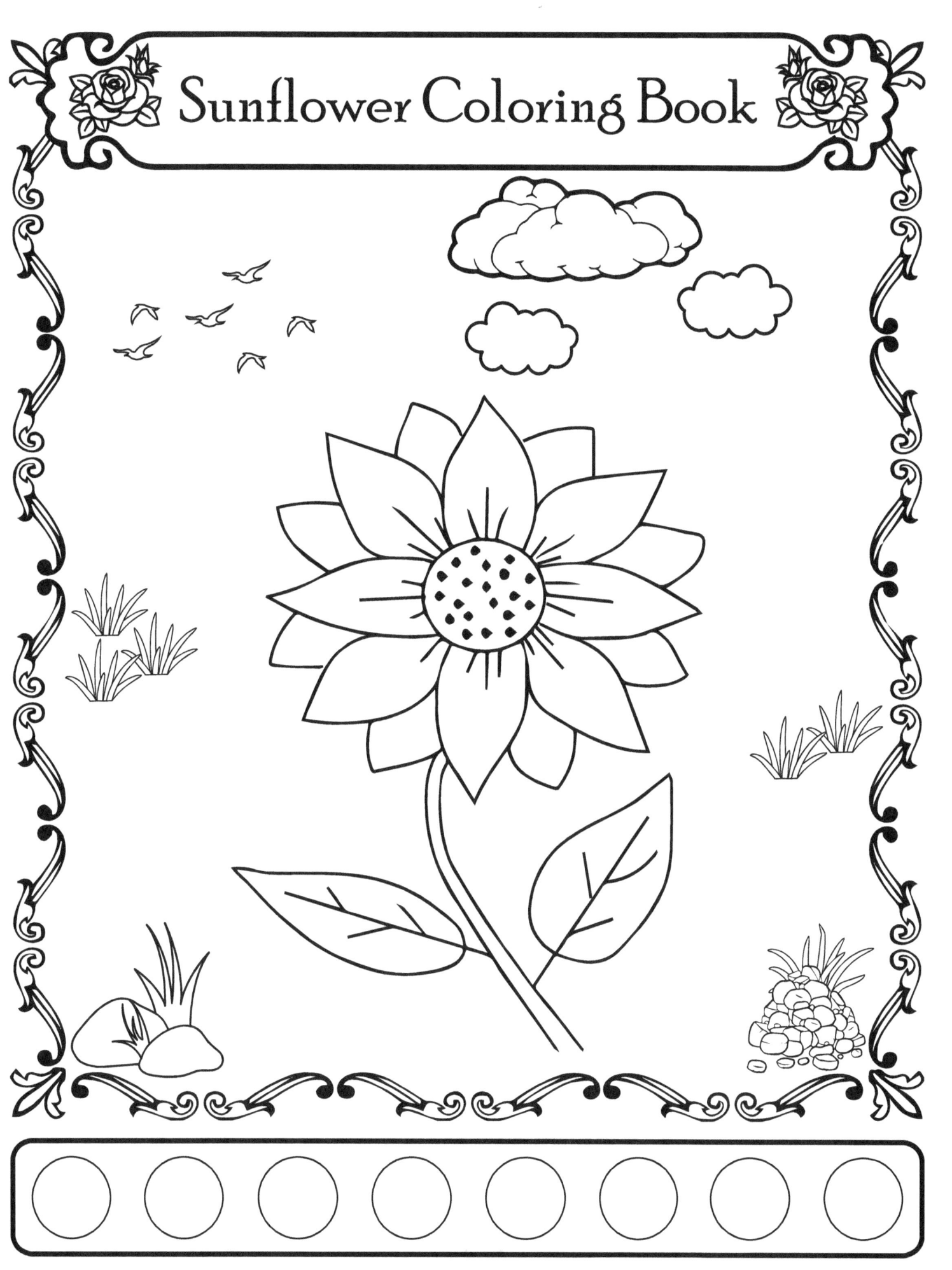

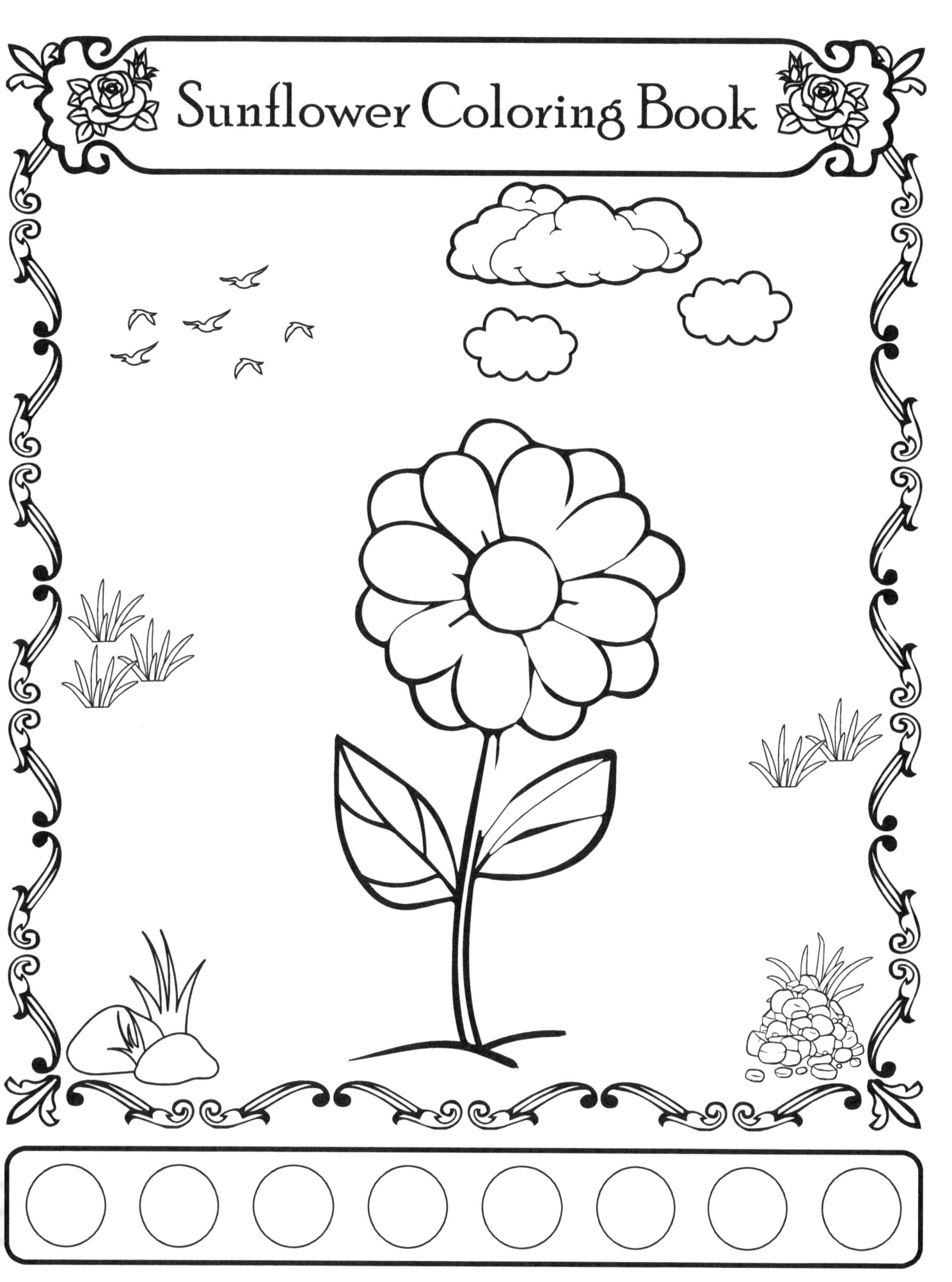

Sunflower Coloring Book

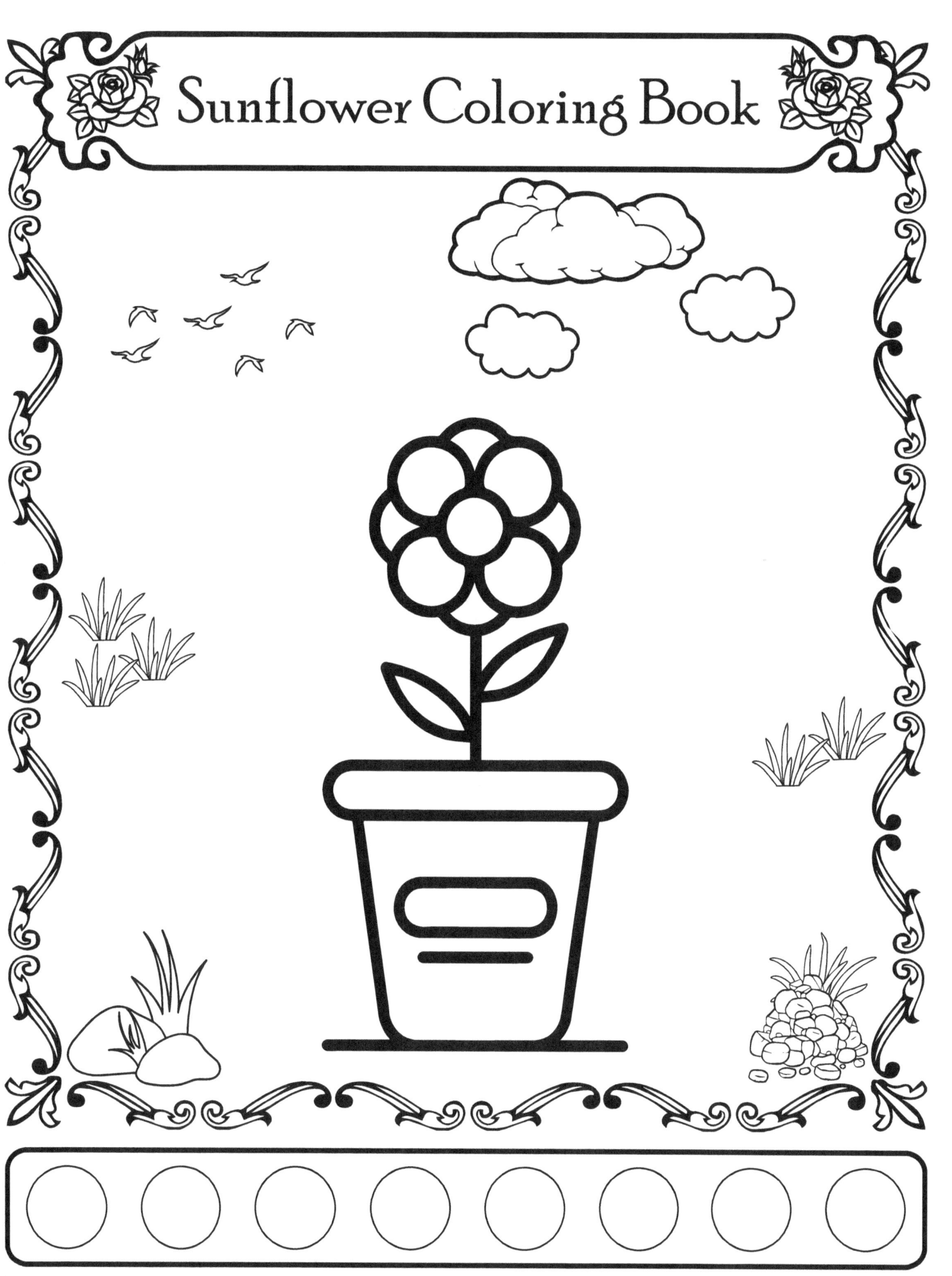

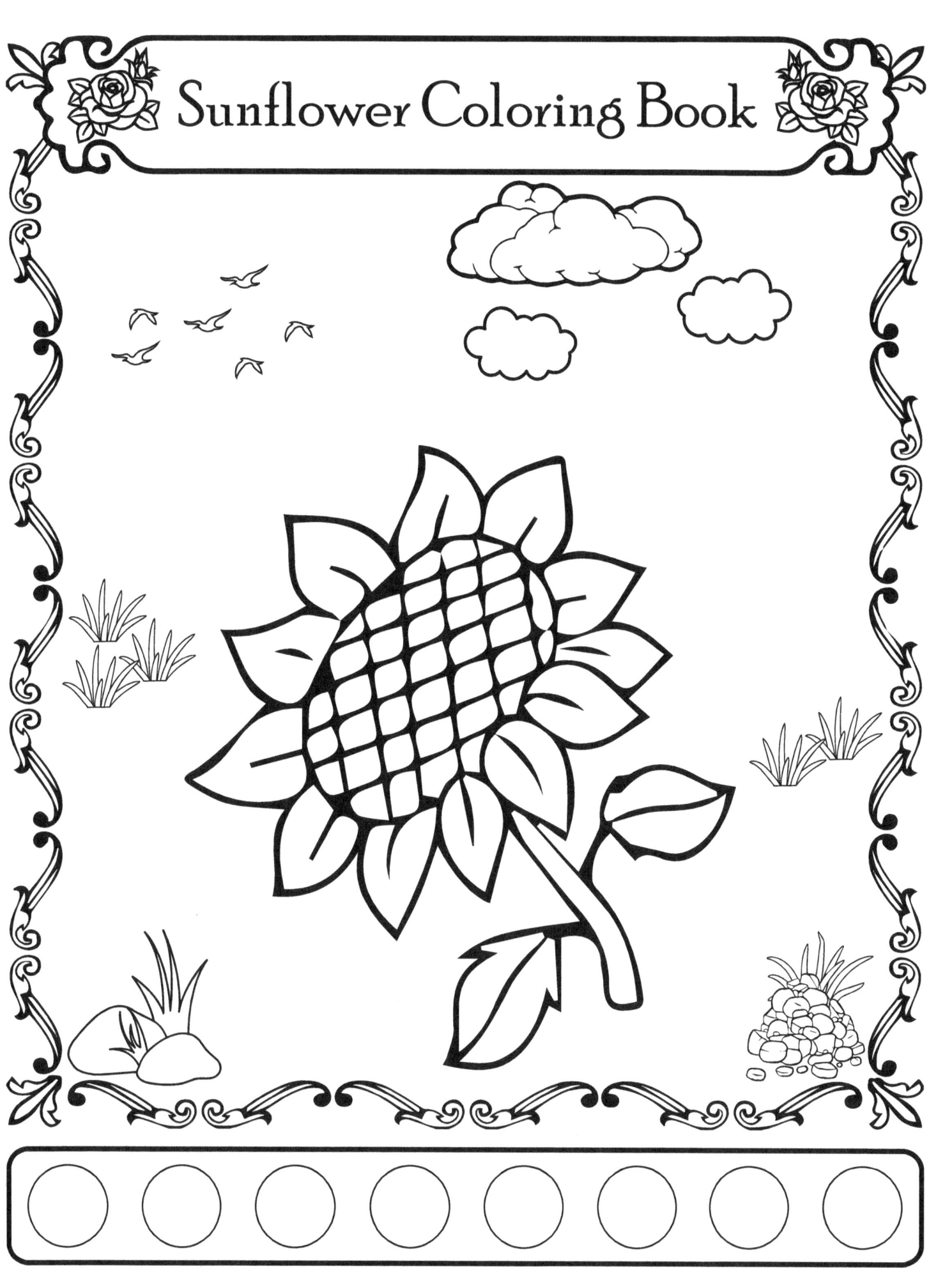

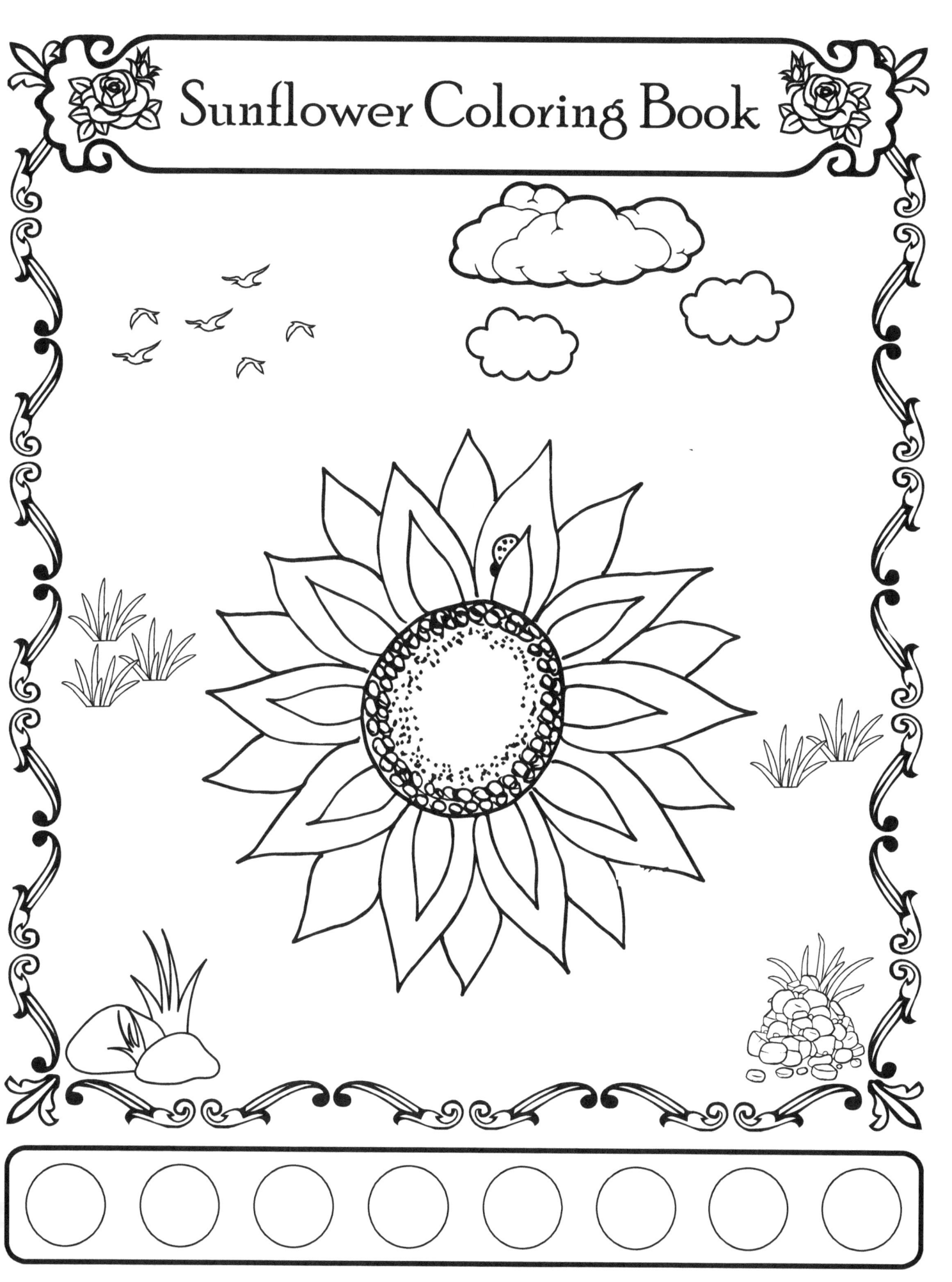

www.ingramcontent.com/pod-product-compliance
Lightning Source LLC
Chambersburg PA
CBHW081656220526
45466CB00009B/2781